WEALTH

A Beginner's Guide to Private Wealth

ADELLA PASOS

Contents

Introduction

Creating wealth is a goal that many people have, but it is not always clear how to achieve it. Building wealth requires a combination of knowledge, discipline, and a solid plan. This book is designed to provide you with the information and tools you need to start creating wealth and reach your financial goals.

Overview of Wealth Creation

Wealth creation is the process of building and growing your assets over time. This can be achieved through a combination of earning more money, saving and investing, and making smart financial decisions.

There are many different strategies for creating wealth, but some of the most effective include:

- Investing in the stock market
- Starting or investing in a business
- Real estate investing
- Saving and budgeting
- Reducing debt

Creating wealth is not just about having more money, it's about having the financial freedom to make choices that align with your values and goals. It's about having the ability to do what you want, when you want, without worrying about money.

Why is Wealth Creation Important

Creating wealth is important for several reasons. First, it provides a sense of security and peace of mind. When you have enough money to meet your needs, you don't have to worry about financial stress and uncertainty. Second, having wealth allows you to have more control over your time. You can choose to work because you want to, not because you have to.

Third, having wealth allows you to have more opportunities in life. You can travel, pursue hobbies and interests, and take care of your loved ones. You can also give back to your community and make a positive impact on the world. Fourth, wealth creation is important for future generations. It is a way to ensure that your family will be taken care of long after you're gone.

This book will guide you through the process of creating wealth, from understanding the basics to advanced strategies and techniques. With the information and tools provided, you will be equipped to take control of your financial future and start building the wealth you deserve.

It's important to note that the information provided is general in nature and not intended as a substitute for professional advice. It's always recommended that you seek advice from a financial advisor or other professional before making any financial decisions.

CHAPTER 1

The Basics of Creating Private Wealth

The first step in creating private wealth is to understand the basics of personal finance. This includes understanding financial statements and financial ratios, budgeting and cash flow management, and setting financial goals and creating a plan to achieve them.

Financial statements and ratios are tools that can help you understand the financial health of your personal finances. These include balance sheets, income statements, and cash flow statements. By understanding these statements, you can identify areas where you can improve your finances and make better financial decisions. Financial ratios, such as the debt-to-income ratio, can also help you understand your financial situation and identify potential problems.

Budgeting and cash flow management are essential for creating private wealth. A budget is a plan for how you will spend your money, and it is essential for tracking your income and expenses. By creating a budget, you can identify areas where you are overspending and make adjustments to improve your financial situation. Cash flow management is also essential for creating private wealth. This involves understanding how money flows in and out of your life and making sure you have enough money to cover your expenses and save for the future.

Once you have a solid understanding of the basics of personal finance, you can start setting financial goals and creating a plan to achieve them. This includes setting short-term and long-term goals and creating a plan to achieve them. Short-term goals might include paying off debt, saving for an emergency fund, or saving for a down payment on a house. Long-term goals might include saving for retirement, creating a college fund for your children, or leaving an inheritance for future generations.

The next step in creating private wealth is to invest your money. Investing is a way to grow your money over time and achieve your financial goals. There are many different types of investments, and it is important to understand the risks and potential returns of each one. Some of the most common types of investments include stocks, bonds, real estate, and mutual funds.

Stocks are a way to invest in companies and can provide the potential for high returns. However, they are also risky and can result in significant losses. Bonds are a way to lend money to companies or governments and can provide a steady stream of income. However, they are typically less risky than stocks and offer lower returns. Real estate can be a great way to create wealth, but it is also a significant investment and requires a lot of time and effort. Mutual funds are a way to invest in a diversified portfolio of stocks, bonds, and other assets and can be a good option for beginners.

It's important to understand that creating wealth is a long-term game, and it's crucial to have a diversified portfolio of investments. Diversification is a strategy that aims to spread your money across different types of investments to reduce risk. By diversifying your portfolio, you can minimize the impact of any one investment on your overall financial situation.

Tax planning and estate planning are also important aspects of creating private wealth. Tax planning involves understanding tax laws and regulations and using strategies to minimize taxes and maximize deductions. Estate planning is the process of transferring your wealth to future generations. This includes creating a will, setting up trusts, and choosing the right executor.

Risk management and insurance are also important aspects of creating private wealth. Risk management involves identifying and managing potential risks to your financial well-being. This includes protecting yourself and your assets from creditors and lawsuits, and preparing for unexpected events such as natural disasters or job loss. Insurance is a way to protect yourself and your assets from financial loss. Types of insurance include life insurance, health insurance, property and casualty insurance, and liability insurance. It's important to understand the types of insurance available, and choose the right coverage to meet your needs.

Working with professional advisors and service providers can also help you in creating private wealth. Financial advisors and wealth managers can help you create and implement a financial plan, and provide guidance on investment decisions. Accountants, attorneys, and other professionals can help you with tax planning, estate planning, and risk management.

Creating private wealth also involves understanding the role of philanthropy and giving in wealth creation. Philanthropy is the act of giving money, time, or resources to charitable causes and organizations. Impact investing is a form of investing that aims to generate a positive social or environmental impact alongside a financial return. By incorporating philanthropy and impact investing into your wealth creation plan, you can align your finances with your values and make a positive impact on the world.

The Importance of Budgeting and Cash Flow Management

Creating wealth is a goal that many people have, but it is not always clear how to achieve it. Building wealth requires a combination of knowledge, discipline, and a solid plan. One of the most important aspects of creating wealth is budgeting and cash flow management. In this article, we will explore the importance of budgeting and cash flow management and how they can help you achieve your financial goals.

Budgeting is the process of creating a plan for how you will spend your money. It involves tracking your income and expenses and identifying areas where you can cut costs and increase savings. A budget is an essential tool for creating wealth because it allows you to understand where your money is going and make adjustments to improve your financial situation.

Creating a budget is a simple process, but it requires discipline and commitment. The first step is to track your income and expenses. This can be done by keeping receipts, bank statements, and credit card statements. Once you have a clear picture of your income and expenses, you can start creating a budget.

The most important part of creating a budget is to set realistic financial goals. This includes setting short-term and long-term goals and creating a plan to achieve them. Short-term goals might include paying off debt, saving for an emergency fund, or saving for a down payment on a house. Long-term goals might include saving for retirement, creating a college fund for your children, or leaving an inheritance for future generations.

Once you have set your goals, you can start creating a budget. This involves dividing your income into categories such as housing, food, transportation, and savings. It's important to make sure that you are allocating enough money to each category, and that you are not overspending in any one area.

Cash flow management is the process of understanding how money flows in and out of your life and making sure you have enough money to cover your expenses and save for the future. A budget is an essential tool for cash flow management because it allows you to track your income and expenses and make sure you have enough money to cover your bills and save for the future.

Cash flow management also involves understanding the difference between fixed expenses and variable expenses. Fixed expenses are expenses that are the same amount each month, such as rent or mortgage payments. Variable expenses are expenses that change each month, such as food or entertainment. By understanding the difference between fixed and variable expenses, you can make adjustments to your budget to ensure that you have enough money to cover your bills and save for the future.

One of the key benefits of budgeting and cash flow management is that it allows you to have more control over your money. When you have a clear understanding of where your money is going, you can make adjustments to your spending to achieve your financial goals. This includes cutting back on unnecessary expenses, increasing your savings, and investing your money.

Another benefit of budgeting and cash flow management is that it allows you to have more control over your time. When you have a solid financial plan in place, you don't have to worry about money and can focus on the things that are important to you. This includes spending time with your family, pursuing hobbies and interests, and giving back to your community.

Budgeting and cash flow management are also essential for reducing debt. Debt can be a major obstacle to creating wealth, and it's important to understand how to manage it. A budget can help you understand where your money is going and identify areas where you can cut costs and increase savings. This can help you pay off debt faster and reduce the amount of interest you are paying.

Another important aspect of budgeting and cash flow management is understanding the importance of saving and investing. Saving and investing are essential for creating wealth because they allow you to grow your money over time. This includes setting aside money for an emergency fund, saving for retirement, and investing in assets such as stocks, bonds, and real estate. A budget can help you understand how much money you can afford to save and invest each month, and help you make informed investment decisions.

It's also important to note that budgeting and cash flow management are not a one-time process. They require ongoing monitoring and adjustments to ensure that you are on track to achieve your financial goals. This means reviewing your budget regularly, tracking your income and expenses, and making adjustments as necessary.

Example of how to use cash flow management with a salary of $100,000 per year:

1. **Start by creating a budget:** Divide your income into categories such as housing, food, transportation, savings, and other expenses. For example, you may allocate $20,000 for housing, $12,000 for food, $8,000 for transportation, and $30,000 for savings and other expenses.

2. **Track your income and expenses:** Keep track of your income and expenses by keeping receipts, bank statements, and credit card statements. This will allow you to see where your money is going and identify areas where you can cut costs and increase savings.

3. **Identify fixed and variable expenses:** Fixed expenses are expenses that are the same amount each month, such as rent or mortgage payments. Variable expenses are expenses that change each month, such as food or entertainment. By understanding the difference between fixed and variable expenses, you can make adjustments to your budget to ensure that you have enough money to cover your bills and save for the future.

4. **Create an emergency fund:** An emergency fund is a savings account that you can use to cover unexpected expenses. Aim to save at least 3-6 months of living expenses in case of job loss, medical emergency or any other unexpected events.

5. **Pay off high-interest debt:** High-interest debt, such as credit card debt, can be a significant obstacle to creating wealth. Prioritize paying off high-interest debt, as it can save you money in the long run and improve your credit score.

6. **Invest in yourself and your future:** Invest in yourself and your future by allocating a portion of your income for education, professional development, and retirement savings.

7. **Review and adjust your budget:** Regularly review and adjust your budget to ensure that you are on track to achieving your financial goals. This means reviewing your budget regularly, tracking your income and expenses, and making adjustments as necessary.

Setting financial goals and creating a plan to achieve them

One of the most important aspects of creating wealth is setting financial goals and creating a plan to achieve them. In this article, we will explore how to set financial goals and create a plan to achieve them in order to become wealthy.

Setting financial goals is the first step in creating wealth. Financial goals are specific, measurable, and time-bound objectives that you want to achieve with your money. They can be short-term or long-term and should align with your values and priorities.

Short-term financial goals might include paying off debt, saving for an emergency fund, or saving for a down payment on a house. Long-term financial goals might include saving for retirement, creating a college fund for your children, or leaving an inheritance for future generations.

When setting financial goals, it's important to be realistic and specific. This means setting goals that are achievable and have a clear deadline. For example, instead of setting a goal to "save more money," set a goal to "save $20,000 for a down payment on a house within the next two years."

Once you have set your financial goals, the next step is to create a plan to achieve them. This involves understanding your current financial situation and identifying the steps you need to take to reach your goals.

One of the most important aspects of creating a plan to achieve your financial goals is understanding your income and expenses. This includes creating a budget, tracking your income and expenses, and identifying areas where you can cut costs and increase savings. By understanding your income and expenses, you can make adjustments to your spending and increase your savings.

Another important aspect of creating a plan to achieve your financial goals is understanding the importance of saving and investing. Saving and investing are essential for creating wealth because they allow you to grow your money over time. This includes setting aside money for an emergency fund, saving for retirement, and investing in assets such as stocks, bonds, and real estate. A budget can help you understand how much money you can afford to save and invest each month, and help you make informed investment decisions.

Creating a plan also involves understanding the importance of risk management and insurance. Risk management is the process of identifying and managing potential risks to your financial well-being. This includes protecting yourself and your assets from creditors and lawsuits, and preparing for unexpected events such as natural disasters or job loss. Insurance is a way to protect yourself and your assets from financial loss. Types of insurance include life insurance, health insurance, property and casualty insurance, and liability insurance. It's important to understand the types of insurance available, and choose the right coverage to meet your needs.

Working with professional advisors and service providers can also help you in achieving your financial goals. Financial advisors and wealth managers can help you create and implement a financial plan, and provide guidance on investment decisions. Accountants, attorneys, and other professionals can help you with tax planning, estate planning, and risk management.

It's also important to note that creating a plan to achieve your financial goals is an ongoing process. This means regularly reviewing your plan, tracking your progress, and making adjustments as necessary.

Top financial goals for people who want to become wealthy

Do any of these sound familiar? It's important to note that these goals may vary depending on an individual's personal financial situation and priorities. These are general goals that can be tailored according to one's needs and goals. It's also important to understand that achieving these goals will take time, effort, and discipline, and it's crucial to have a plan to achieve them and to seek professional advice when needed.

- Pay off high-interest debt
- Build an emergency fund
- Create a budget and stick to it
- Increase income through a career change or side hustle
- Save for a down payment on a house
- Max out retirement accounts
- Create a college fund for children or grandchildren
- Invest in a diversified portfolio of stocks, bonds, and real estate
- Create a will and estate plan
- Reduce taxes through strategic tax planning
- Increase credit score

- Create multiple streams of passive income
- Invest in yourself through education and professional development
- Reduce unnecessary expenses
- Give back to the community through philanthropy

World's Wealthiest People and How They Became Wealthy

It's important to note that this list is based on the net worth as of 2023, and this is subject to change as the economy fluctuates. Additionally, these individuals come from a variety of backgrounds and industries, but they all share a common thread of hard work, dedication, and a willingness to take risks and think outside the box.

Elon Musk - The CEO of SpaceX and Tesla, Elon Musk has a net worth of over $200 billion. He made his fortune through a combination of technology and innovation. He founded and sold PayPal, the online payment system, and has been instrumental in the success of SpaceX and Tesla, which have revolutionized the space and automotive industries.

Jeff Bezos - The founder and CEO of Amazon, Jeff Bezos has a net worth of over $150 billion. He started Amazon as an online bookstore in 1994 and has grown it into one of the largest and most successful e-commerce companies in the world.

Bill Gates - The co-founder of Microsoft, Bill Gates has a net worth of over $130 billion. He co-founded Microsoft in 1975 and has been instrumental in its success, making it the world's largest personal-computer software company.

Bernard Arnault - The CEO of LVMH, Bernard Arnault has a net worth of over $110 billion. He is the chairman and CEO of LVMH, the world's largest luxury-goods company, which owns brands such as Louis Vuitton, Dior, and Bulgari.

Mark Zuckerberg - The co-founder and CEO of Facebook, Mark Zuckerberg has a net worth of over $100 billion. He co-founded Facebook in 2004 and has grown it into one of the largest and most successful social media companies in the world.

Warren Buffett - The CEO of Berkshire Hathaway, Warren Buffett has a net worth of over $90 billion. He is widely considered to be one of the most successful investors in history, and has built his fortune through a combination of smart investments and successful business acquisitions.

Larry Ellison - The co-founder of Oracle, Larry Ellison has a net worth of over $80 billion. He co-founded Oracle in 1977 and has grown it into one of the largest and most successful software companies in the world.

Larry Page - The co-founder of Google, Larry Page has a net worth of over $70 billion. He co-founded Google in 1998 and has grown it into one of the largest and most successful internet companies in the world.

Sergey Brin - The co-founder of Google, Sergey Brin has a net worth of over $65 billion. He co-founded Google in 1998 and has grown it into one of the largest and most successful internet companies in the world.

Mukesh Ambani - The chairman and largest shareholder of Reliance Industries, Mukesh Ambani has a net worth of over $60 billion. He inherited the company from his father, and has grown it into one of the largest and most successful companies in India, with interests in energy, petrochemicals, textiles, natural resources, retail, and telecommunications.

CHAPTER 2

Investment Strategies of the Wealthy

It's important to note that different types of investments come with different levels of risk and potential return. It's important to do your research and understand the potential risks and rewards before investing. Additionally, it's also important to diversify your investments across different types of assets, sectors, and geographies to mitigate the risk of a single investment affecting your overall portfolio. Work with a financial advisor, who can help you create a personalized wealth creation strategy that aligns with your financial goals and risk tolerance.

People are getting wealthy from investments by earning a return on their money through the buying and selling of assets such as stocks, bonds, real estate, and other financial products. Investing allows individuals to grow their wealth over time, as the returns on their investments can be greater than the interest earned from savings accounts or other low-risk investments. Additionally, investing allows individuals to diversify their assets, spreading risk across a variety of investments rather than relying on one source of income.

There are various types of private wealth investments that individuals can make to grow their wealth, including:

Stocks: Investing in stocks allows individuals to own a small piece of a company and share in the company's profits. When the company performs well, the stock price increases and the investor can sell their shares for a profit.

Bonds: Investing in bonds is essentially lending money to a government or corporation. The bond issuer pays the investor interest and returns the principal when the bond matures.

Real estate: Investing in real estate can include buying rental properties, investing in real estate development, or participating in a real estate investment trust (REIT). Real estate investments can generate income through rental payments and appreciation in property value.

Commodities: Investing in commodities such as gold, silver, oil, and agricultural products can be a way to diversify a portfolio and potentially profit from price changes.

Private equity: Investing in private equity involves buying shares in privately held companies that are not listed on the stock market. This can include venture capital, buyout funds, and hedge funds. Private equity can generate significant wealth, but it also involves a higher level of risk.

Mutual funds: Investing in mutual funds is a way to invest in a diverse portfolio of stocks, bonds, and other securities. These funds are managed by professional investors, who make the investment decisions on behalf of the fund's shareholders.

Cryptocurrency: Investing in digital currencies such as Bitcoin and Ethereum. These are decentralized forms of digital currency that are not controlled by a central authority. They are traded on various platforms and can be highly volatile in terms of value.

Art or Collectibles: Investing in art or collectibles can lead to wealth by providing the opportunity for appreciation in value over time. Many types of art and collectibles, such as paintings, sculptures, rare books, coins, and stamps, have a history of increasing in value as they age. This is known as the "investment potential" of art or collectibles. As the demand for these items increases over time, so does their value.

Starting a business: Starting a business can lead to wealth by creating an income stream that is not dependent on a salary or wages. Business owners have the potential to earn unlimited income based on the success of their business. They can also increase their wealth through reinvesting profits into the business for growth and expansion.

Inventing or patenting a product: Inventing or patenting a product and licensing it can generate significant wealth. This can lead to future income through royalties. Patent holders can collect royalties from anyone who uses their patent, and inventors can collect royalties from anyone who uses or sells their invention. This can provide a steady stream of income for the patent holder or inventor over time.

Investing in start-ups: Investing in start-ups can be a high-risk, high-reward strategy for generating wealth. If a start-up company becomes successful, the value of the investment can increase significantly. This can lead to substantial returns for the investors, and provide a path to significant wealth. However, it's important to keep in mind that not all start-ups are successful and investors should be prepared to lose their entire investment. Due diligence and professional advice should be sought before making such investments.

Investing in a franchise: Investing in a franchise can be a relatively low-risk way to generate wealth, as the franchisor has already established a successful business model. If a franchisee is able to effectively operate and grow the business, they can enjoy a steady stream of income and potentially significant returns on investment. However, it's important to note that the success of a franchise depends on various factors such as the location, competition, and the franchisee's ability to operate and manage the business effectively.

Investing in a hedge fund: Investing in a hedge fund can generate significant wealth, but it also involves a higher level of risk. Investing in a hedge fund can be a way to potentially generate significant wealth through the use of sophisticated investment strategies, such as short selling, leverage and derivatives. Hedge funds are typically managed by experienced investment professionals who aim to generate returns that are not correlated with the stock market or other traditional investments.

Here are other methods people used to become wealthy and earn passive income royalties:

Earning royalties can be a valuable way to generate a steady stream of passive income, which can help to provide financial stability and allow for long-term wealth building. Additionally, earning royalties allows you to leverage your assets to generate income, and has the potential for significant growth in wealth over time.

It's important to note that earning royalties from these sources may require significant investment, research and development, and marketing to turn it into a profitable business. Additionally, it's also important to seek professional advice when looking into earning royalties, as some of the options may have different legal and tax implications.

Licensing a patent or trademark: Licensing your patent or trademark to other companies allows them to use your invention or brand in exchange for a fee.

Publishing a book or music: Authors and songwriters can earn royalties from the sale of their books or music.

Creating and selling a course: If you create and sell an online course, you can earn royalties from each sale.

Renting out property: Landlords can earn royalties from rent paid by tenants.

Investing in a royalty trust: Investing in a royalty trust allows individuals to earn royalties from the sale of natural resources such as oil or gas.

Royalties from mineral rights: If you own the rights to minerals on your property, you can earn royalties from the extraction of those minerals.

Franchising a business: Franchisees pay royalties to the franchisor for the right to use the franchisor's name, business model, and other intellectual property.

Creating and selling a software: If you create and sell a software, you can earn royalties from each sale.

Renting out equipment: Renting out equipment, such as oil drilling equipment, can generate royalties.

Investing in a royalty partnership: Investing in a royalty partnership allows individuals to earn royalties from the sale of products such as pharmaceuticals.

Creating and selling a mobile app: If you create and sell a mobile app, you can earn royalties from each sale or through in-app purchases.

Licensing a product design: Licensing your product design to other companies allows them to use your design in exchange for a fee.

Creating and selling a video game: If you create and sell a video game, you can earn royalties from each sale.

Creating and selling a theme park ride: If you create and sell a theme park ride, you can earn royalties from each ride installed in a theme park.

Creating and selling a jingle or theme song: If you create and sell a jingle or theme song, you can earn royalties from its use in commercials, movies, and television shows.

Creating and selling a website template: If you create and sell a website template, you can earn royalties from each sale.

Licensing a photograph or illustration: If you license your photographs or illustrations to other companies or individuals, you can earn royalties from each use.

Creating and selling a script: If you create and sell a script, you can earn royalties from its use in movies, television shows, and plays.

Creating and selling a recipe: If you create and sell a recipe, you can earn royalties from its use in cookbooks and food products.

Creating and selling a plugin for a software: If you create and sell a plugin for a software, you can earn royalties from each sale of the plugin.

Creating and selling stock footage: If you create and sell stock footage, you can earn royalties from each use of the footage.

Licensing a character or brand: If you license a character or brand, you can earn royalties from its use in merchandise, movies, and television shows.

Creating and selling a font: If you create and sell a font, you can earn royalties from its use in design and publishing.

Creating and selling a virtual reality or augmented reality experience: If you create and sell a virtual reality or augmented reality experience, you can earn royalties from each sale.

Creating and selling a software as a service (SaaS): If you create and sell a software as a service, you can earn royalties from monthly or yearly subscription fees.

Creating and selling a podcast: If you create and sell a podcast, you can earn royalties from sponsorships, ads, and subscriber fees.

Creating and selling a video tutorial: If you create and sell a video tutorial, you can earn royalties from each sale or subscription fees.

Creating and selling a fitness program: If you create and sell a fitness program, you can earn royalties from each sale or subscription fees.

Creating and selling a mobile game: If you create and sell a mobile game, you can earn royalties from in-game purchases, ads, and subscription fees.

Creating and selling a plugin for a website: If you create and sell a plugin for a website, you can earn royalties from each sale.

Licensing a logo or branding: If you license your logo or branding to other companies or individuals, you can earn royalties from each use.

Creating and selling a language learning app: If you create and sell a language learning app, you can earn royalties from each sale or subscription fees.

Creating and selling a recipe app: If you create and sell a recipe app, you can earn royalties from in-app purchases, ads, and subscription fees.

Creating and selling a graphic design template: If you create and sell a graphic design template, you can earn royalties from each sale.

Licensing a theme for a website or blog: If you license a theme for a website or blog, you can earn royalties from each use.

Creating and selling a virtual event or conference: If you create and sell a virtual event or conference, you can earn royalties from registration or ticket fees.

Creating and selling a theme for a mobile app: If you create and sell a theme for a mobile app, you can earn royalties from each sale.

Creating and selling a 3D model or animation: If you create and sell a 3D model or animation, you can earn royalties from each sale or licensing agreement.

Creating and selling a virtual reality game or experience: If you create and sell a virtual reality game or experience, you can earn royalties from each sale or subscription fees.

Creating and selling a print on demand product, such as t-shirts, mugs, or phone cases: If you create and sell a print on demand product, you can earn royalties from each sale.

Creating and selling a stock audio: If you create and sell stock audio, you can earn royalties from each use of the audio.

Creating and selling a theme or template for a website or mobile app: If you create and sell a theme or template, you can earn royalties from each sale.

Creating and selling a stock music: If you create and sell stock music, you can earn royalties from each use of the music.

Creating and selling a stock 3D assets: If you create and sell stock 3D assets, you can earn royalties from each use of the assets.

Creating and selling stock sound effects: If you create and sell stock sound effects, you can earn royalties from each use of the sound effects.

Creating and selling a stock virtual instrument: If you create and sell stock virtual instruments, you can earn royalties from each use of the instruments.

Creating and selling stock photographs: If you create and sell stock photographs, you can earn royalties from each use of the photographs.

Creating and selling stock vector illustrations: If you create and sell stock vector illustrations, you can earn royalties from each use of the illustrations.

Creating and selling stock 3D models : If you create and sell stock 3D models, you can earn royalties from each use of the models.

Creating and selling a stock stock 3D animations: If you create and sell stock 3D animations, you can earn royalties

Earning royalties can be a valuable source of income for those looking to become wealthy. The benefits of earning royalties include a steady stream of passive income, as royalties are typically paid out on a regular basis, such as monthly or quarterly. This can help provide financial stability and allow for long-term wealth building. Additionally, earning royalties allows you to leverage your assets, such as patents, trademarks, or creative works, to generate income without having to actively sell or promote the product or service.

Another benefit of earning royalties is the potential for significant growth in wealth over time. As the demand for the product or service increases, so does the potential for higher royalties. Additionally, many forms of royalties, such as those from patents, have the potential to generate income for many years, even decades, providing a long-term source of income. Furthermore, royalties can also be a way to diversify your income streams, which can help to mitigate the risk of relying too heavily on one source of income.

Using Asset Allocation and Diversification of Investments to Build Wealth

Asset allocation and diversification are two key strategies for building wealth through investing. Asset allocation refers to the process of dividing an investment portfolio among different asset categories, such as stocks, bonds, and cash. The goal of asset allocation is to distribute investments among different types of assets in a way that aligns with an investor's risk tolerance and financial goals. By spreading investments among different asset classes, investors can potentially reduce the overall risk of their portfolio.

Diversification, on the other hand, refers to the process of spreading investments among different individual securities within an asset class. For example, an investor might diversify their stock investments by buying shares in different companies, sectors, and geographic regions. The goal of diversification is to reduce the risk of a portfolio by spreading investments among a variety of different securities. This way, if one security performs poorly, the portfolio's overall performance is less likely to be negatively affected.

When used together, asset allocation and diversification can be powerful tools for building wealth through investing. By spreading investments among different asset classes and individual securities, investors can potentially reduce the overall risk of their portfolio, while still having the opportunity for growth. It's important to note that diversification and asset allocation do not guarantee a profit or protect against loss, and investors should consider their own risk tolerance and financial goals before making any investment decisions. Additionally, it's always recommended to seek professional advice before making any decisions on how to invest your money.

How to Understand and Evaluate Different Investment Vehicles

When it comes to understanding and evaluating different investment vehicles, it's important to understand the basics of each type of investment. Stocks, for example, represent ownership in a company, and the value of a stock can fluctuate based on the performance of the company and the broader market. Bonds, on the other hand, represent a loan to a company or government, and the value of a bond can fluctuate based on interest rates and the creditworthiness of the borrower.

Real estate investments, meanwhile, can take the form of rental properties, REITs, or other types of real estate-based investments, and the value of real estate can fluctuate based on a number of factors, including location, economic conditions, and changes in the housing market.

When evaluating different investment vehicles, it's important to consider the risks and potential returns of each option. For example, stocks can offer the potential for higher returns, but also come with higher risk. Bonds, on the other hand, tend to be less volatile, but also offer lower returns. Real estate investments can offer steady income streams, but also come with the risk of fluctuations in property values and the costs of maintenance and repairs.

It's also important to consider how different investment vehicles fit into your overall investment strategy and financial goals. **For example, if you're looking for a steady stream of income, bonds or rental properties might be a better fit than stocks. If you're willing to take on more risk in exchange for potentially higher returns, stocks might be a better fit.** It's important to have a well-diversified portfolio that aligns with your risk tolerance and financial goals, and it's always recommended to seek professional advice before making any investment decisions.

10 Types of Investments that are generally considered to be steady for streams of income:

Bonds: Bonds are debt securities issued by governments, municipalities, or corporations. They generally pay a fixed interest rate and the principal is returned at maturity.

Dividend-paying stocks: Some companies pay dividends to their shareholders, which provide a steady stream of income.

Real estate investment trusts (REITs): REITs are companies that own and operate income-producing real estate and are required by law to distribute a certain percentage of their income to shareholders as dividends.

Certificates of Deposit (CDs): CDs are low-risk, fixed-income investments offered by banks and credit unions. They pay a fixed interest rate and are FDIC insured.

Peer-to-peer lending: Peer-to-peer lending platforms match borrowers with investors who provide loans. Investors earn interest on their loans and can earn a steady stream of income.

Annuities: Annuities are insurance products that provide a steady stream of income in exchange for an upfront payment or series of payments.

Rental properties: owning rental properties can provide a steady stream of income through rental payments.

High-yield savings accounts and money market funds: These investments offer a low-risk way to earn a steady stream of interest income.

Infrastructure investment funds: Infrastructure investment funds invest in assets such as highways, bridges, and airports, that generate income through user fees or tolls.

Agricultural investment funds: Agricultural investment funds invest in assets such as farmland, that generate income through crop yields or rent.

10 Investment Strategies That are Commonly Used By The Wealthy

Diversification: spreading investments among different asset classes and individual securities to reduce overall portfolio risk.

Alternative investments: investing in assets such as real estate, private equity, and hedge funds that are not typically found in traditional investment portfolios.

Active management: actively managing a portfolio through buying and selling individual securities, as opposed to a passive approach like index investing.

Hedging: using financial instruments such as options and futures to protect against potential losses in other parts of the portfolio.

Tax-efficient investing: structuring investments in a tax-efficient manner to minimize the impact of taxes on investment returns.

Asset protection: using legal structures and insurance to protect assets from potential liabilities.

Private banking: utilizing the services of a private bank for wealth management and specialized financial services.

Impact investing: investing in companies, funds, or projects that aim to generate positive social or environmental impact, as well as financial return.

Philanthropy: using a portion of wealth for charitable giving, either through direct donations or through the use of charitable vehicles such as foundations or donor-advised funds.

Intergenerational wealth transfer: planning for the transfer of wealth to future generations through estate planning and trusts.

CHAPTER 3

Creating Multiple Streams of Income

Creating multiple streams of income is a common strategy among wealthy individuals for generating wealth and building financial security. This can include a variety of income-generating activities such as investing in stocks, bonds, and real estate, starting a business, earning royalties, or renting out properties. By diversifying their income streams, wealthy individuals can potentially reduce the overall risk of their financial portfolio and increase their earning potential.

One way wealthy people create multiple streams of income is through **investing in a variety of assets.** For example, they might invest in stocks, bonds, real estate, and alternative investments such as private equity or hedge funds. Each of these asset classes has the potential to generate income through dividends, interest, or rental income. Additionally, they may also invest in a variety of individual securities within each asset class to further diversify their portfolio.

Another way wealthy people create multiple streams of income is through **starting their own business or investing in existing businesses.** This can include starting a new business from scratch, buying into an existing business, or investing in a franchise. This can provide a steady stream of income through profits and can also offer significant growth potential.

Furthermore, wealthy people may also earn royalties from patents, trademarks, or creative works, and rent out properties for additional income streams. Creating multiple streams of income is a common strategy among wealthy individuals for generating wealth and building financial security. This can include a variety of income-generating activities such as investing in stocks, bonds, and real estate, starting a business, earning royalties, or renting out properties **(as mentioned in the previous chapter)**. By diversifying their income streams, wealthy individuals can potentially reduce the overall risk of their financial portfolio and increase their earning potential.

Additionally, consider diversifying within each asset class by investing in a variety of individual securities. It's also important to consider your risk tolerance, time horizon and financial goals while making these investments.

In addition to these, **there are other ways to create multiple streams of income such as consulting, teaching, writing, and creating digital products.** Keep in mind that creating multiple streams of income is not a one-time event, it's a continuous process that requires regular monitoring, evaluation and adjustments.

When deciding how to create multiple streams of income, it's important to consider your goals, risk tolerance, and resources. It's also important to remember that diversifying your income streams is not a guarantee of financial success, and it's always recommended to seek professional advice before making any investment decisions.

Benefit of Having Multiple Streams of Income

Having multiple streams of income is important for several reasons. First and foremost, it helps to diversify your income and reduce risk. By having multiple sources of income, you are less reliant on any one source, which can provide a level of financial security and peace of mind. This is particularly important in today's economy where job security and income stability can be uncertain.

Secondly, having multiple streams of income can help you to reach your financial goals faster. With multiple streams of income, you have the potential to earn more money overall, which can help you to save more, invest more, and achieve your financial goals more quickly. This can be especially beneficial for those looking to achieve financial independence or retire early.

Finally, having multiple streams of income can provide a sense of financial flexibility. With multiple streams of income, you have the ability to pursue different opportunities and interests, whether that means starting a business, investing in real estate, or pursuing a side hustle. This can provide a sense of financial freedom and the ability to live the life you want. Additionally, having multiple streams of income can also provide a sense of purpose and fulfillment, as you're not just relying on one source of income, but you're actively working towards building different income streams.

Having multiple streams of income is important as it helps to diversify your income, reduce risk, reach financial goals faster, and provides financial flexibility and fulfillment. However, it's important to keep in mind that creating multiple streams of income requires effort, planning and monitoring, and it's always recommended to seek professional advice before making any investment decisions.

CHAPTER 4

How to Protect Your Wealth from Taxes

Protecting your wealth from taxes is an important aspect of financial planning. Taxes can significantly reduce the amount of money you have to save and invest, and they can also increase the amount of time it takes to reach your financial goals. By understanding the tax implications of your financial decisions, you can take steps to minimize your tax burden and keep more of your money working for you.

One of the main reasons why it's important to protect your wealth from taxes is that taxes can significantly erode your investment returns. For example, if you earn a 10% return on your investments but pay a 30% tax rate, your net return is only 7%. By minimizing your tax burden, you can potentially increase your investment returns and reach your financial goals more quickly.

Another reason why it's important to protect your wealth from taxes is that taxes can make it more difficult to save and invest for the future. When you have to pay a significant portion of your income in taxes, you have less money available to save and invest. This can make it more difficult to reach your financial goals, such as saving for retirement or buying a home.

There are several ways to protect your wealth from taxes, such as:

- Investing in tax-advantaged accounts such as 401(k)s, IRAs, and HSAs.

- Maximizing deductions and credits such as the mortgage interest deduction, charitable giving, and state and local tax deductions.

- Using legal entities such as limited liability companies (LLCs) and family limited partnerships (FLPs) to minimize taxes on business income.

- Investing in tax-free municipal bonds.

- Setting up a trust to minimize estate taxes and to ensure that assets are passed on to beneficiaries in a tax-efficient manner.

- Offshore banking and investing in countries with lower tax rates.

- Establishing a tax domicile in a state or country with lower taxes.

- Creating a charitable foundation or charitable trust to support causes and receive tax benefits.

- Utilizing cost segregation studies to reclassify assets and accelerate depreciation for tax purposes.

- Investing in real estate and utilizing depreciation, cost segregation and 1031 exchanges to defer taxes.

- Using a self-directed solo 401(k) or self-directed IRA to invest in real estate or other alternative assets tax-free.

- Utilizing a life insurance policy as a tax-efficient way to pass on wealth to beneficiaries.

- Using charitable remainder trusts to generate income and receive tax benefits.

- Creating a pension plan for self-employed individuals

- Using a Roth IRA conversion ladder

- Creating and using a private annuity trust

- Investing in real estate and utilizing deductions and depreciation

- Setting up a Self-Directed Real Estate IRA

- Utilizing a Self-Directed IRA LLC
- Investing in a Qualified Opportunity Zone Fund
- Investing in a Qualified Business Income Deduction
- Utilizing the Foreign Earned Income Exclusion
- Using a Self-Directed Checkbook Control IRA
- Creating a Self-Directed Roth IRA
- Investing in a Qualified Small Business Stock
- Utilizing the Section 199A Qualified Business Income Deduction
- Utilizing a Health Savings Account
- Investing in a Qualified Longevity Annuity Contract
- Setting up a Self-Directed Roth 401(k)
- Utilizing the Capital Gains Tax Bracket
- Utilizing a Self-Directed SEP IRA
- Setting up a private foundation
- Utilizing a Roth Conversion Ladder
- Investing in a Master Limited Partnership
- Utilizing the Foreign Tax Credit
- Investing in a Qualified Opportunity Fund
- Utilizing the Foreign Earned Income Exclusion
- Using a Self-Directed Solo 401(k)
- Creating a Self-Directed Checkbook Control IRA
- Investing in a Qualified Small Business Stock
- Utilizing the Section 199A Qualified Business Income Deduction
- Utilizing a Health Savings Account

- Investing in a Qualified Longevity Annuity Contract
- Utilizing the Capital Gains Tax Bracket
- Utilizing a Personal Residence Trust
- Using a foreign tax credit to offset taxes paid to foreign governments
- Investing in tax-free municipal bonds
- Utilizing the step-up in basis at death to reduce capital gains taxes
- Creating a charitable remainder trust
- Using a charitable lead trust
- Utilizing the lifetime gift tax exclusion
- Investing in a Qualified Opportunity Fund
- Utilizing the Foreign Earned Income Exclusion
- Using a Qualified Personal Residence Trust
- Investing in a Qualified Small Business Stock
- Utilizing a Self-Directed IRA
- Using a Health Savings Account
- Investing in a Qualified Longevity Annuity Contract
- Utilizing the Foreign Tax Credit
- Utilizing the Section 199A Qualified Business Income Deduction
- Using a family office or wealth management firm to manage investments and tax strategy.
- Keeping informed on tax laws and regulations and consulting with a tax professional or financial advisor to plan finances in a tax-efficient way.

- Working with a tax professional or financial advisor to plan your finances in a tax-efficient way

It's also important to keep in mind that taxes, laws and regulations are subject to change and it's always recommended to keep informed and seek professional advice. Protecting your wealth from taxes is important as it can significantly erode your investment returns, make it more difficult to save and invest for the future and it's essential to keep informed and seek professional advice to plan your finances in a tax-efficient way. I would recommend consulting with a tax attorney or certified financial planner for accurate and up-to-date information on how to protect your wealth from taxes.

How Wealthy People Use Life Insurance to Save on Taxes and Profit

It's important to note that tax laws are subject to change, and it's always advisable to consult with a tax professional to understand how using life insurance policies can save on taxes and how it applies to your specific situation.

Premiums paid on life insurance policies are tax-deductible: Wealthy individuals can deduct the premiums paid on their life insurance policies from their taxable income. This can help to reduce the overall amount of taxes they owe.

Tax-free death benefit: The death benefit from a life insurance policy is generally tax-free. This means that when a policyholder dies, their beneficiaries will not have to pay taxes on the death benefit they receive. This can be a significant advantage for wealthy individuals who want to pass on their wealth to their beneficiaries without the burden of taxes.

Life insurance trusts: Wealthy individuals can use life insurance trusts to hold their life insurance policies and avoid estate taxes on the death benefit. These trusts can also be used to protect assets from creditors and lawsuits.

Charitable giving: Life insurance can also be used as a charitable giving tool. A wealthy individual can donate a life insurance policy to a charity and receive a tax deduction for the policy's cash value. The charity can then use the death benefit to fund their programs.

Business planning: Business owners can also use life insurance policies to save on taxes by creating buy-sell agreements. These agreements provide a way to transfer ownership of the business in case of death or disability.

Wealthy individuals can use life insurance to profit in a few different ways. One way is by using a technique called **"life insurance arbitrage" or "insurance premium financing",** where the wealthy individual takes out a large life insurance policy and borrows money from the policy's cash value to invest in other assets. This allows the individual to invest in assets that have a higher expected return than the cost of the insurance policy, effectively earning a profit.

Another way wealthy individuals can use life insurance to profit is by **using it as a tool for estate planning and tax management**. By owning a life insurance policy, they can pass on wealth to their beneficiaries tax-free. Additionally, they can also use life insurance to fund a trust, which can be used to protect their assets from creditors and lawsuits.

Lastly, wealthy individuals can also use **life insurance as a way to generate an income stream**. Some life insurance policies, such as annuities, can be used to provide a steady stream of income in exchange for a lump sum investment. This income stream can be used to supplement retirement income or to fund other investments.

Which Life Insurance Policies Generate Income?

There are several types of life insurance policies that can generate income, including:

Whole life insurance: This type of policy provides a death benefit and also builds cash value over time, which can be borrowed against or used to pay premiums.

Universal life insurance: Similar to whole life insurance, universal life insurance also builds cash value over time, but it typically has more flexibility in terms of premium payments and death benefit amounts.

Variable life insurance: This type of policy allows the policyholder to invest the cash value in a variety of investment options, such as stocks and bonds. The returns on these investments can provide additional income for the policyholder.

Indexed Universal Life: This type of policy allows the policyholder to invest the cash value in an indexed account which is tied to a stock market index such as S&P500. The returns on these investments can provide additional income for the policyholder.

It's important to note that using life insurance for profit may require a significant amount of investment and might not be suitable for everyone, and should be discussed with a financial advisor before making any decisions.

CHAPTER 5

Risk Management &
Estate Planning for Your Investments

How does it feel to lose money on investments?

Wealthy individuals usually have a variety of feelings about losing money on their investments. Some may feel a sense of disappointment or frustration, while others may view it as a learning opportunity or a temporary setback.

One thing to keep in mind is that wealthy individuals typically have a higher net worth and more diversified portfolio of investments, which may cushion the impact of losing money on a specific investment. This could make them less emotionally affected by losing money on their investments. Additionally, many wealthy individuals have a long-term perspective on their investments and may be less focused on short-term fluctuations in the market. They may view losing money on an investment as a temporary setback and a part of the normal volatility of the markets.

However, it's important to note that wealthy people may also have more at stake and more to lose, so they may be more cautious and diligent in risk management strategies to mitigate the potential losses. It's also important to keep in mind that every person is different and how they react to losing money on their investments can vary based on their individual personality, risk tolerance, financial goals, and experiences.

Sometimes it's just a temporary setback or they may be more cautious and diligent in risk management strategies to mitigate the potential losses in the future. Conducting risk management for your investments is an essential part of creating and preserving wealth. Risk management is the process of identifying and evaluating potential risks that could negatively impact your investments, and taking steps to mitigate or eliminate those risks. By conducting proper risk management, you can potentially reduce the chances of losing money on your investments and increase the chances of achieving your financial goals.

One of the main reasons why risk management is important is that it can help you avoid large losses. By identifying and evaluating potential risks, you can take steps to avoid investments that are too risky or to reduce your exposure to those risks. This can help you avoid large losses that could set you back significantly in your quest to build wealth.

Another reason why risk management is important is that it can help you achieve your financial goals. By identifying and mitigating risks, you can potentially increase your chances of achieving your financial goals, such as saving for retirement or buying a home. This is because you will have a better understanding of the risks that you are taking and be able to make more informed investment decisions.

There are several ways to conduct risk management for your investments, such as:

- Diversifying your investments across different asset classes, sectors and geographies
- Monitoring your investments and making adjustments as needed
- Working with a financial advisor or professional to evaluate and manage risks
- Regularly reviewing and updating your financial plan
- Staying informed about the market and economic trends

It's important to keep in mind that risk management is not a one-time event but a continuous process that requires regular monitoring, evaluation and adjustments.

Conducting risk management for your investments is important because it can help you avoid large losses, achieve your financial goals and it's a continuous process that requires regular monitoring, evaluation and adjustments. Additionally, it's always recommended to seek professional advice and stay informed about the market and economic trends.

Where Can You Buy Risk Management Services for Wealth?

Wealth management firms: These firms typically offer a wide range of services, including financial planning, investment management, and risk management. They often work with high net worth individuals and families to create customized investment portfolios and risk management strategies.

Insurance companies: Many insurance companies offer risk management services to high net worth individuals and families, including personal liability insurance, personal umbrella insurance, and other types of coverage to protect their assets and wealth.

Investment banks: Investment banks may offer risk management services to high net worth individuals and families, including risk assessments, portfolio evaluations, and customized hedging strategies.

Private banks: Private banks often offer risk management services to high net worth individuals and families, such as asset protection, tax and estate planning, and other financial services.

Financial advisors: Financial advisors can offer risk management services to wealthy clients and provide them with a comprehensive financial plan that takes into account the client's risk tolerance and investment goals.

Hedge funds and other alternative investment firms: These firms may offer specialized risk management services to high net worth individuals and families, such as hedge funds and other alternative investments.

Consulting firms: Some consulting firms offer risk management services to high net worth individuals and families, including risk assessments, portfolio evaluations, and customized hedging strategies.

It's important to keep in mind that not all providers are created equal and it's always recommended to do a thorough research and seek professional advice to find the right provider that fits your needs and goals.

How Does Estate Planning Services Protect My Wealth?

Estate planning is an important aspect of protecting your wealth for the long-term. It involves creating a plan for how your assets will be distributed after you die, and it can help ensure that your wealth is passed on to your loved ones in the most efficient and tax-advantaged way possible.

One of the main benefits of estate planning is that it can help you minimize estate taxes. Estate taxes are taxes that are imposed on the transfer of assets from one generation to the next. By creating an estate plan, you can potentially reduce or eliminate estate taxes, which can help preserve more of your wealth for your loved ones.

Estate planning also helps you to have control over the distribution of your assets, even after you pass away. With a well-drafted will or trust, you can ensure that your assets are distributed according to your wishes and not the laws of the state you reside in. This can be particularly important if you have children from a previous marriage or if you want to provide for someone with special needs.

Another benefit of estate planning is that it can help protect your assets from creditors and lawsuits. By creating a trust, for example, you can potentially protect your assets from creditors and lawsuits and ensure that your loved ones are provided for after you pass away.

Estate planning can also help you plan for incapacity. If you were to become incapacitated and unable to make decisions for yourself, a durable power of attorney and a health care proxy can ensure that someone you trust is able to make decisions on your behalf and according to your wishes.

Example of Estate Planning for Wealthy

Let's say a wealthy individual named John wants to ensure that his assets are passed on to his children and grandchildren in the most tax-efficient way possible. John meets with an estate planning attorney who helps him create a plan that includes the following elements:

1. **A Living Trust:** John creates a living trust that holds the majority of his assets, including his investments, real estate, and business interests. This allows him to transfer these assets to his children and grandchildren without having to go through the probate process.

2. **A Will:** John also creates a will that states how he wants his remaining assets to be distributed. The will also names a guardian for his minor children and an executor to manage the distribution of his assets.

3. **A Durable Power of Attorney:** John creates a durable power of attorney that names his oldest son as his agent to manage his financial affairs in the event that he becomes incapacitated.

4. **A Health Care Proxy:** John also creates a health care proxy, which names his wife as his agent to make medical decisions on his behalf in case he is unable to do so.

5. **Gift and Tax Planning:** John's attorney helps him with gift and tax planning to minimize the estate taxes. He makes gifts of cash and assets to his children and grandchildren and set up

a charitable remainder trust which would provide income to his wife and reduce the value of his estate.

By implementing these estate planning tools, John is able to ensure that his assets are passed on to his loved ones in the most tax-efficient way possible. The living trust and will allow his assets to be distributed without going through probate, the durable power of attorney and health care proxy ensure that his affairs are managed according to his wishes, and the gift and tax planning help him reduce the estate taxes.

It's important to note that this is just one example and estate planning strategies can vary based on an individual's specific needs and goals. It's always recommended to seek professional advice from an estate attorney to ensure that your estate plan is legally sound and tailored to your specific needs and goals.

CHAPTER 6

Leaving an inheritance for your children

It's important to keep in mind that every person is different and the reasons why they may choose to leave an inheritance for their children can vary based on their individual personality, values, financial goals, and beliefs. Leaving an inheritance for children is a way to provide them with financial security and stability, pass on values, create opportunities, preserve family legacy and for estate tax planning. It's always recommended to seek professional advice and have a comprehensive plan that includes estate planning, tax planning and wealth management strategies. These are the top reasons people tend to leave an inheritance for their children:

Providing financial security: One of the main reasons why wealthy individuals leave an inheritance for their children is to provide them with financial security and stability. An inheritance can provide children with a financial cushion, which can help them achieve their own financial goals, such as buying a home, starting a business, or saving for retirement.

Passing on values: Many wealthy individuals view leaving an inheritance as a way to pass on their values and beliefs to their children. By leaving an inheritance, they can help ensure that their children understand the importance of hard work, responsibility, and the value of money.

Creating opportunities: An inheritance can create opportunities for children that they might not otherwise have. For example, an inheritance can provide the funds for a child to pursue higher education or to start their own business.

Preserving family legacy: Many wealthy individuals view leaving an inheritance as a way to preserve their family legacy. They may want to ensure that their family name and legacy continue for future generations.

Estate tax planning: Leaving an inheritance can also be a way for wealthy individuals to reduce their estate taxes. By transferring assets to their children, they can potentially reduce the size of their estate, which can lower the amount of estate taxes that will be due.

There are several steps a wealthy person can take to get the inheritance process started:

Create an estate plan: The first step in getting the inheritance process started is to create an estate plan. This typically involves working with an estate planning attorney to create a will, a trust, and other documents that will outline how your assets will be distributed after you pass away.

Identify your assets and liabilities: The next step is to identify all of your assets and liabilities. This includes property, investments, bank accounts, businesses, and any other assets you may have. It's important to also identify any debts or liabilities that you may have, so that they can be taken into account when creating your estate plan.

Make a list of beneficiaries: Once you have identified your assets and liabilities, you should make a list of beneficiaries. This includes the people or organizations you want to inherit your assets after you pass away.

Review and update your estate plan regularly: It's important to review and update your estate plan regularly, as your assets and liabilities, as well as the laws and regulations, can change over time.

Communicate your plan with your beneficiaries: It's important to communicate your plan to your beneficiaries, this will help them understand your wishes and how your assets will be distributed after you pass away.

Consult with a tax and financial advisor: It's also important to work with a tax and financial advisor who can assist you in creating an estate plan that takes into account your tax and financial goals and can also help you with tax planning.

Implement your plan: Once your estate plan is complete, the next step is to implement it by transferring assets into trust, gifting assets and making other necessary arrangements as outlined in your plan.

FAQ about Inheritance Planning:

How can I plan for the distribution of my assets if I have children from different marriages?

If you have children from different marriages, it's important to consider how you want your assets to be distributed among them in your estate plan. Here are some steps you can take to plan for the distribution of your assets in this situation:

Create a will: Create a will that clearly states how you want your assets to be distributed among your children. This will ensure that your wishes are followed after you pass away.

Consider using a trust: Consider using a trust to hold your assets. This can give you more control over the distribution of your assets and can also provide tax benefits. You can create different trusts for different children or create a trust that distributes assets to your children at different ages or under certain conditions.

Review and update your estate plan regularly: It's important to review and update your estate plan regularly, as your assets and liabilities, as well as the laws and regulations, can change over time.

Communicate your plan with your children: It's important to communicate your plan to your children, this will help them understand your wishes and how your assets will be distributed after you pass away.

Consult with an attorney and a financial advisor: Seek professional advice from an estate attorney and a financial advisor who can assist you in creating an estate plan that takes into account your specific needs and goals, and who can also help you with tax planning.

Consider a prenuptial agreement if you remarry: If you remarry, you may also want to consider a prenuptial agreement that lays out how your assets will be divided in the event of a divorce or death.

How can I plan for the distribution of my digital assets?

It's important to keep in mind that laws and regulations around digital assets can vary from state to state, and it's always recommended to seek professional advice from an attorney and/or a financial advisor to ensure that your plan is legally sound and tailored to your specific needs and goals.

Make a list of your digital assets: Make a list of all your digital assets, including online bank accounts, digital currency, email accounts, social media accounts, online storage accounts, and any other digital assets you may have.

Update your will or trust: Make sure to include your digital assets in your will or trust and make sure that your executor or trustee has the necessary information to access and manage them.

Use a digital asset management service: Consider using a digital asset management service, which can help you store and manage your digital assets and provide a way for your beneficiaries to access them after you pass away.

Use a password manager: Use a password manager to store your login information and passwords for your digital assets, and make sure that your executor or trustee has access to them.

Provide instructions on how to access your assets: Provide your executor or trustee with clear instructions on how to access your digital assets, including login information and passwords, and any other information they may need to access them.

Review and update your plan regularly: Review and update your plan regularly, as laws and regulations around digital assets can change over time.

Identify a digital executor: Appoint someone you trust as your digital executor, that person will be responsible for managing and distributing your digital assets according to your instructions.

Keep your devices and accounts active: Keep your devices and accounts active, in case you pass away your loved ones will have an easier time accessing your digital assets.

How can I plan for the distribution of my assets if I live abroad?

Understand the laws of the country you live in: It's important to understand the laws of the country you live in, as they can affect how your assets are distributed after you pass away. Make sure to consult with a local attorney to understand the laws and regulations around inheritance, estate planning and taxes.

Create a will: Create a will that clearly states how you want your assets to be distributed among your beneficiaries. Make sure that your will is valid under the laws of the country you live in, and also under the laws of any country where you own assets.

Understand the laws of the countries where you own assets: If you own assets in more than one country, it's important to understand the laws of each country, as they can affect how your assets are distributed. Make sure to consult with attorneys in each country to understand the laws and regulations around inheritance, estate planning and taxes.

Consider using a trust: Consider using a trust to hold your assets. This can give you more control over the distribution of your assets and can also provide tax benefits. Trusts can be particularly useful for holding assets in different countries, as they can help you navigate the different laws and regulations.

Review and update your estate plan regularly: It's important to review and update your estate plan regularly, as your assets and liabilities, as well as the laws and regulations, can change over time.

Communicate your plan with your beneficiaries: It's important to communicate your plan to your beneficiaries, this will help them understand your wishes and how your assets will be distributed after you pass away.

Consult with an attorney and a financial advisor: Seek professional advice from an estate attorney and a financial advisor who can assist you in creating an estate plan that takes into account your specific needs and goals, and who can also help you with tax planning.

CHAPTER 7

How to protect your assets
from creditors and lawsuits

Wealthy people often take steps to protect their assets from creditors and lawsuits for a number of reasons. One of the main reasons is to ensure that their assets are not seized to pay off debts or judgments. Additionally, protecting assets can also help maintain privacy, as well as allow for more control over the distribution of assets in the event of death or incapacity.

Here are some ways that wealthy people can protect their assets from creditors and lawsuits:

Use Asset Protection Trusts: One of the most common ways wealthy people protect their assets is by creating an asset protection trust. This type of trust is designed to protect assets from creditors and lawsuits by placing them in a trust that is controlled by a trustee. The assets are no longer owned by the individual, and therefore cannot be seized by creditors or litigants.

LLCs and Corporations: Setting up a limited liability corporation (LLC) or a corporation can also be a good way to protect assets from creditors and lawsuits. These entities provide liability protection for the owners, making it more difficult for creditors or litigants to access the assets of the company.

Use Retirement Accounts: Retirement accounts, such as IRAs and 401(k)s, are typically protected from creditors and lawsuits. This means that if a wealthy person has a significant amount of money invested in these types of accounts, it can provide a level of protection for their assets.

Purchase Umbrella Insurance: Purchasing an umbrella insurance policy can provide additional liability protection for the wealthy person's assets. This type of insurance policy provides extra coverage above and beyond the limits of the individual's regular insurance policies.

Keep the assets in different jurisdictions: Wealthy people may also choose to keep their assets in different jurisdictions, such as offshore accounts or foreign property, as the laws and regulations in different countries can vary, and this can make it more difficult for creditors or litigants to access the assets.

Use Pre-Nuptial Agreements: If the wealthy person is married or is planning to get married, a prenuptial agreement can be an effective way to protect assets from creditors and lawsuits. This type of agreement lays out how assets will be divided in the event of a divorce or death.

Use Family Limited Partnerships (FLP): A Family Limited Partnership (FLP) is a legal entity that can be used to hold and manage assets. FLP's can provide liability protection for the assets and make it more difficult for creditors or litigants to access them.

Use Homestead laws: Some states have homestead laws that protect a certain amount of equity in a person's primary residence from creditors. Wealthy people can take advantage of these laws to protect a portion of their assets.

Use Tenancy by the entirety: Tenancy by the entirety is a type of property ownership that is only available to married couples. It allows both spouses to have an undivided interest in the property and provides protection from creditors and lawsuits.

Use Offshore Asset Protection Trusts: Offshore Asset Protection Trusts are similar to domestic asset protection trusts, but they are established in a foreign jurisdiction, and they can provide even greater protection from creditors and lawsuits, as the laws and regulations can be different from the home country.

CHAPTER 8

The Do's and Don'ts of Wealth

Wealth can be a powerful tool that can help individuals achieve their goals and live the life they want. However, managing wealth can also be complex, and there are certain do's and don'ts that should be followed in order to ensure that wealth is used effectively and responsibly.

The Do's of Wealth:

Do set financial goals: One of the most important things to do when managing wealth is to set clear financial goals. This can help individuals stay focused and motivated, and can also help them make better decisions about how to use their wealth.

Do create a budget: A budget can be a powerful tool for managing wealth, as it can help individuals understand where their money is going and make sure they are using it in the most effective way.

Do invest in a diverse range of assets: Diversifying investments is one of the most important things to do when managing wealth. This can help individuals spread risk and maximize returns.

Do seek professional advice: Wealth management can be complex, and it's important to seek professional advice from financial advisors, attorneys, and other experts to ensure that wealth is being used effectively and responsibly.

Do have an estate plan: Having a well-designed estate plan in place is an essential step for protecting your wealth and ensuring that it is passed on to your loved ones in the most efficient way possible.

Do protect your assets from creditors and lawsuits: It's important to take steps to protect your assets from creditors and lawsuits, as this can help ensure that your wealth is not seized to pay off debts or judgments.

Do leave an inheritance for your children: Leaving an inheritance for your children can help ensure that they are provided for financially, and can also be a way to pass on your values and legacy to future generations.

Do save and invest: Building wealth is not only about earning a high income, but also spending less than you earn, and saving and investing the difference.

The Don'ts of Wealth:

Don't make impulsive decisions: It's important to think carefully about how to use wealth and avoid making impulsive decisions. This can help ensure that wealth is used effectively and responsibly.

Don't neglect budgeting and cash flow management: Neglecting budgeting and cash flow management can lead to financial problems and make it more difficult to achieve financial goals.

Don't put all your eggs in one basket: Avoid putting all your wealth in one investment or one type of investment, as it can put your wealth at risk if the investment doesn't perform well.

Don't neglect estate planning: Neglecting estate planning can lead to complications and financial difficulties for your loved ones after you pass away, and may result in unnecessary taxes and fees.

Don't neglect risk management: Neglecting risk management can lead to significant financial losses, so it's important to understand and manage risks associated with your investments.

Don't neglect tax planning: Neglecting tax planning can result in paying more taxes than necessary and can also lead to financial difficulties in the long term.

Don't neglect your financial education: Neglecting your financial education can lead to poor decision-making and make it more difficult to achieve financial goals. It's important to continuously learn and educate yourself on financial matters.

Don't ignore the importance of multiple streams of income: Relying solely on one source of income can make you vulnerable to financial shocks. Building multiple streams of income can provide a safety net and a way to build wealth over time.

Remember! Managing wealth is not just about accumulating money, but also about making sure that it's being used effectively and responsibly. By following the do's and don'ts of wealth, individuals can make better decisions about how to use their wealth and achieve their financial goals. It's important to seek professional advice and continuously educate yourself about financial matters. Remember to set financial goals, create a budget, diversify investments, protect assets, plan for the future, manage risks and think long-term.

CHAPTER 9

Creating a plan for
Philanthropy and Giving Back

Creating a plan for philanthropy is an important step for wealthy individuals who want to make a positive impact on the world and give back to their communities. Philanthropy can take many forms, from giving money to charitable organizations, to volunteering time and skills, to making a difference through advocacy and policy change. Regardless of the form it takes, philanthropy can provide significant benefits to the wealthy, both personally and professionally.

One of the main reasons why wealthy individuals should create a plan for philanthropy is because it can help them make a meaningful difference in the world. Philanthropy allows individuals to support causes and organizations that align with their values and passions, and to have a direct impact on the lives of people in need. Whether it's supporting education and healthcare initiatives, fighting poverty and inequality, or protecting the environment, philanthropy allows individuals to make a real difference in the world.

Another benefit of philanthropy for the wealthy is that it can help them build a legacy. Philanthropy can be a way for individuals to leave a lasting impact on the world, and to be remembered for the good they have done. It can also be a way to pass on values and a sense of social responsibility to future generations.

Philanthropy can also provide personal benefits for the wealthy. Giving back can be a fulfilling and rewarding experience, and can help individuals feel a sense of purpose and meaning in their lives. It can also be a way to connect with others and build relationships within their communities.

Philanthropy can also have professional benefits for the wealthy. Giving back can help individuals build their reputation and standing within their communities and industries. It can also be a way to gain exposure and recognition for their businesses, and to build relationships with other leaders and influencers.

Creating a plan for philanthropy also allows the wealthy to be strategic in their giving. It's important to understand the causes and organizations that align with the individual's values, and what the specific needs are for those causes. Furthermore, it allows the wealthy to measure the impact of their giving and make adjustments as needed.

However, it's important to note that philanthropy should not be used as a replacement for paying one's fair share of taxes. Philanthropy should be viewed as an additional way for the wealthy to give back to their community, not as a way to avoid paying taxes.

Another important aspect to consider when creating a plan for philanthropy is to be mindful of the potential impact of their giving. It's important to consider whether their giving will have a lasting positive impact and whether it will empower the communities they are trying to support rather than creating dependency.

Remember! Philanthropy can provide significant benefits to the wealthy, both personally and professionally. It allows individuals to make a meaningful difference in the world, build a legacy, gain personal fulfillment, and build their reputation and standing. However, it's important to create a plan for philanthropy that aligns with the individual's values, and to be mindful of the potential impact of their giving. It's also important to not use philanthropy as a replacement for paying one's fair share of taxes. Philanthropy can be a powerful tool for making a difference in the world, but it should be used responsibly and strategically.

What is an example of a philanthropy plan?

An example philanthropy plan can take many forms, depending on the individual's goals, values, and resources. However, a basic structure for a philanthropy plan may include the following elements:

Mission statement: A clear statement of the individual's values and goals for their philanthropy, and what causes and organizations they want to support.

Giving priorities: A list of the specific causes and organizations the individual wants to support, and why they have chosen those causes and organizations.

Giving strategy: A plan for how the individual will give, including the type of giving (financial, time, skills), the amount of giving, and the frequency of giving.

Impact measurement: A plan for how the individual will measure the impact of their giving, and how they will evaluate and adjust their giving strategy as needed.

Communication and engagement: A plan for how the individual will communicate and engage with the causes and organizations they support, and how they will involve their family and friends in their philanthropy.

Estate planning and legacy giving: A plan for how the individual will include philanthropy in their estate and legacy giving, and how they will pass on their values and legacy to future generations.

An example of a philanthropy plan for an individual might look like this:

Mission statement: To support education and healthcare initiatives that empower underprivileged communities, and to promote sustainable development and environmental conservation.

Giving priorities:

Supporting education and healthcare initiatives in underprivileged communities through financial donations to organizations such as UNICEF and Save the Children.

Investing in renewable energy and sustainable development through impact investing in companies and funds that promote sustainable energy solutions.

Supporting environmental conservation and biodiversity through financial donations to organizations such as WWF and The Nature Conservancy.

Giving strategy:

Donating 1% of annual income to education and healthcare initiatives, and 1% of annual income to environmental conservation and sustainable development.

Investing 5% of investable assets in impact investments that promote sustainable energy solutions.

Volunteering time and skills to support education and healthcare initiatives through mentorship and volunteering programs.

Impact measurement:

Tracking the impact of donations on education and healthcare initiatives, and measuring the impact of sustainable energy investments.

Regularly reviewing and evaluating the effectiveness of the giving strategy and making adjustments as needed.

Communication and engagement:

Staying informed and engaged with the causes and organizations supported through regular communication and updates.

Inviting family and friends to join in philanthropic activities and encouraging them to support similar causes.

Estate planning and legacy giving:

Including philanthropy as a priority in estate planning and legacy giving to ensure that the values and goals of philanthropy are passed onto future generations.

It's important to note that this is just one example of a philanthropy plan, and that there are many different ways to structure a plan depending on the individual's goals, values, and resources. It's recommended to work with a financial advisor and an attorney to ensure that the plan is legally sound and tailored to the individual's specific needs and goals.

Some of the most common giving priorities among wealthy individuals include:

Education: Many wealthy individuals are passionate about supporting education initiatives, such as providing scholarships, funding schools, or building educational infrastructure in underprivileged communities.

Health and Medical Research: Supporting health and medical research is also a common giving priority for wealthy individuals. This includes funding for disease research and supporting hospitals and clinics.

Poverty and Hunger: Many wealthy individuals choose to support organizations that fight poverty and hunger, both domestically and internationally.

Arts and Culture: Many wealthy individuals are interested in supporting the arts, such as museums, theater, and music.

Environment: Wealthy individuals are often interested in supporting causes related to the environment, such as conservation, renewable energy, and sustainable development.

Human Rights: Wealthy individuals are also passionate about supporting human rights initiatives, such as organizations that support refugees, children, and women's rights.

Animal welfare: Some wealthy individuals are passionate about supporting animal welfare initiatives, such as funding animal shelters and protecting wildlife.

Community Development: Many wealthy individuals are interested in supporting community development initiatives, such as rebuilding neighborhoods, creating jobs and investing in local businesses

Disaster Relief: Many wealthy individuals choose to support disaster relief organizations, such as the Red Cross, which provide aid to communities affected by natural disasters.

Religious or faith-based initiatives: Many wealthy individuals choose to support religious or faith-based initiatives, such as building churches, funding religious schools, and supporting mission trips.

Again, it's important to note that this is not an exhaustive list and that wealthy individuals giving priorities can vary greatly depending on their personal values, passions, and experiences.

Top 25 Most Common Giving Strategies of the Wealthy

It's important to note that this list is not exhaustive and that there are many different ways to give back, and that wealthy individuals can combine multiple strategies to create a giving plan that aligns with their values and goals.

Financial donations: One of the most common giving strategies for wealthy individuals is to make financial donations to charitable organizations and causes that align with their values and passions.

Impact investing: Wealthy individuals may also choose to invest in companies and funds that align with their values and promote social and environmental impact.

Philanthropic advising: Many wealthy individuals seek out philanthropic advising to help them identify and evaluate giving opportunities and create a giving strategy that aligns with their values and goals.

Donor-advised funds: Donor-advised funds (DAFs) allow wealthy individuals to make a charitable contribution and receive an immediate tax deduction, while retaining the ability to recommend grants from the fund over time.

Private foundations: Private foundations allow wealthy individuals to make a significant charitable contribution and have more control over how the funds are used, often with the goal of having a long-term impact.

Charitable trusts: Charitable trusts allow wealthy individuals to make a charitable contribution and receive a tax deduction, while also providing an income stream for themselves or their beneficiaries.

Charitable gift annuities: Charitable gift annuities allow wealthy individuals to make a charitable contribution, receive a tax deduction, and receive a fixed income stream in return.

Charitable remainder trusts: Charitable remainder trusts allow wealthy individuals to make a charitable contribution, receive a tax deduction, and receive an income stream in return, while also providing a benefit to the charity at the end of the trust term.

Charitable lead trusts: Charitable lead trusts allow wealthy individuals to make a charitable contribution, receive a tax deduction, and provide an income stream to the charity for a period of time, with the remainder going to the individual or their beneficiaries.

Social enterprise: Wealthy individuals may also choose to create a social enterprise, which is a business that aims to achieve a social or environmental impact alongside financial returns.

Volunteering: Some wealthy individuals choose to give back by volunteering their time and skills to organizations that align with their values and passions.

Cause-related marketing: Some wealthy individuals choose to give back by aligning their business with a cause and making a donation based on sales or other business activities.

Matching gifts: Some wealthy individuals choose to give back by matching the charitable contributions of their employees, family, or friends.

Employee giving programs: Some wealthy individuals choose to give back by setting up employee giving programs, which allow employees to make charitable contributions through payroll deductions.

Advocacy and policy change: Some wealthy individuals choose to give back by advocating for and supporting policy changes that align with their values and passions.

Community involvement: Some wealthy individuals choose to give back by getting involved in their local communities, such as serving on non-profit boards, organizing charity events, or participating in community service projects.

Sponsorship: Some wealthy individuals choose to give back by sponsoring events or organizations that align with their values and passions.

Art and collectibles donation: Some wealthy individuals choose to give back by donating their art and collectibles to museums, libraries, and other cultural institutions.

Pro bono work: Some wealthy individuals choose to give back by providing pro bono services such as legal, accounting, or consulting services to non-profit organizations.

Environmental conservation: Some wealthy individuals choose to give back by investing in conservation, such as protecting endangered species, preserving natural habitats, or supporting sustainable agriculture.

Innovative giving: Some wealthy individuals choose to give back by creating new and innovative ways of giving, such as crowdfunding, online giving platforms, or mobile giving apps.

Collaboration: Some wealthy individuals choose to give back by collaborating with other philanthropists and donors, by creating giving circles, sharing resources, or co-funding initiatives.

Education grants: Some wealthy individuals choose to give back by providing education grants to underprivileged students or funding educational programs in developing countries.

Support research: Some wealthy individuals choose to give back by funding research in fields such as medicine, technology, and science.

Preservation of cultural heritage: Some wealthy individuals choose to give back by supporting the preservation of cultural heritage, such as funding the restoration of historical buildings, artifacts, and landmarks.

CHAPTER 10

Choosing the right financial advisors for wealth

When it comes to managing your wealth, it's essential to work with the right financial advisors. Choosing the right advisors can help you make informed decisions about your money and achieve your financial goals. But with so many financial advisors to choose from, it can be challenging to know where to start. Here are some key factors to consider when choosing the right financial advisors for wealth management:

Credentials and qualifications: One of the most important factors to consider when choosing a financial advisor is their credentials and qualifications. Look for advisors who hold relevant professional designations such as Certified Financial Planner (CFP), Chartered Financial Analyst (CFA), or Chartered Financial Consultant (ChFC). These designations indicate that the advisor has met certain education and experience requirements and has passed an exam in their field of expertise.

Experience and track record: It's also important to consider an advisor's experience and track record. Look for advisors who have been in the business for a significant amount of time and have a proven track record of helping clients achieve their financial goals.

Services offered: Different financial advisors offer different services, so it's essential to understand what services an advisor can provide. Some advisors specialize in investment management, while others may focus on tax planning or estate planning. Be sure to choose an advisor who can provide the services you need.

Investment philosophy: It's important to understand an advisor's investment philosophy and how it aligns with your own. Look for advisors who have a clear and consistent investment philosophy, and who are willing to explain it to you in a way that you can understand.

Fees and compensation: Be sure to understand how an advisor is compensated and what fees they charge. Some advisors charge a flat fee, while others charge a percentage of assets under management. It's essential to choose an advisor whose fees and compensation structure aligns with your own financial goals.

Communication and accessibility: Finally, it's essential to choose an advisor who is easy to communicate with and accessible when you need them. Look for advisors who are responsive to your questions and concerns and who are willing to make themselves available to you when you need them.

By considering these factors, you can make an informed decision about the right financial advisors for your wealth management needs. It's also important to do your own research, ask for references and meet with several advisors before making a final decision. Remember that building a good relationship with your financial advisor is key to achieving your financial goals and it's important to feel comfortable and confident in their ability to help you make informed decisions about your wealth.

Common challenges of the Wealthy and How to Avoid Them

Maintaining privacy and security: One of the common challenges for the wealthy is maintaining privacy and security for themselves and their families. This can include protecting personal and financial information, as well as physical security for themselves and their property. Strategies for avoiding this challenge include working with trusted advisors, implementing strong security measures, and being discreet about one's wealth.

Managing expectations: Another common challenge for the wealthy is managing the expectations of others, such as friends, family, and business associates. This can include dealing with requests for financial assistance or pressure to maintain a certain lifestyle. Strategies for avoiding this challenge include setting clear boundaries, communicating expectations, and being assertive.

Preserving wealth: Preserving wealth over multiple generations is a common challenge for the wealthy. Strategies to avoid this challenge include estate planning, creating a family mission statement, and implementing wealth transfer strategies.

Investing wisely: One of the common challenges for the wealthy is investing their money wisely. This can include evaluating investment opportunities, avoiding fraud and scams, and diversifying investments to reduce risk. Strategies for avoiding this challenge include working with a financial advisor, conducting thorough research, and diversifying investments.

Balancing work and leisure: Wealthy individuals may face a challenge of balancing their work and leisure time. Strategies for avoiding this challenge include setting clear boundaries between work and leisure, prioritizing relaxation and self-care, and scheduling regular vacations.

Philanthropy: Many wealthy individuals face the challenge of deciding where to direct their philanthropy efforts and how to make the most impact. Strategies to avoid this challenge include research, setting clear goals, and working with a philanthropic advisor.

Dealing with taxes: The wealthy may face challenges when it comes to managing taxes, including understanding tax laws, avoiding audits, and minimizing tax liability. Strategies for avoiding this challenge include working with a tax advisor, creating a tax plan, and implementing tax-efficient investment strategies.

Managing multiple properties: The wealthy may face challenges in managing multiple properties, including maintenance, security, and rental income. Strategies for avoiding this challenge include hiring a property manager, creating a budget, and setting clear expectations with tenants.

Handling lawsuits: The wealthy may face challenges in dealing with lawsuits, including protecting assets and managing reputations. Strategies for avoiding this challenge include working with a lawyer, creating an asset protection plan, and being proactive in resolving disputes.

Managing the next generation: A common challenge for the wealthy is how to prepare and pass on their wealth to the next generation. Strategies for avoiding this challenge include creating a family mission statement, setting clear expectations, and educating the next generation about financial responsibility.

Where Can I Buy Wealth Management Services?

Wealth management services are sold by a variety of financial institutions and professionals. Some of the main providers of wealth management services include:

Banks: Many large banks and regional banks offer wealth management services to their customers. These services often include investment management, estate planning, and trust services.

Brokerage firms: Brokerage firms such as Charles Schwab, TD Ameritrade, Fidelity, and E-Trade also offer wealth management services to their clients. These services include investment management, retirement planning, and tax planning.

Independent financial advisors: Independent financial advisors, also known as Registered Investment Advisors (RIAs), are another option for wealth management services. These advisors are typically fee-based and offer a wide range of services including investment management, retirement planning, tax planning, and estate planning.

Investment management firms: Some firms, such as Blackrock, Vanguard, and Fidelity Investments offer wealth management services. They have a team of investment professionals that manage and monitor the portfolios of high net worth individuals.

Family offices: Some wealthy families set up a family office to manage their wealth. These offices typically provide a wide range of services, such as investment management, tax planning, and estate planning, as well as other services like legal and accounting advice.

Insurance companies: Some insurance companies offer wealth management services, often in the form of annuities, which provide a steady stream of income in exchange for a lump sum investment.

Private banks: Private banks offer wealth management services to high net worth individuals, focusing on providing personalized services like investment management, tax planning, estate planning and trust services.

It's important to note that this is not an exhaustive list and that there are many different providers of wealth management services, and it's important to research and compare different options to find the one that best suits your needs.

Conclusion

In conclusion, achieving financial success and building private wealth is a journey that requires patience, discipline, and a clear plan. Whether you are starting from zero or looking to take your wealth to the next level, the strategies and tips outlined in this book can help you reach your financial goals.

From understanding the basics of budgeting and cash flow management, to setting financial goals and creating a plan to achieve them, to investing in various types of private wealth, this book has provided a comprehensive guide to help you understand the key concepts and strategies involved in building and maintaining wealth. Remember, wealth building is a lifelong process, and it's important to keep learning and growing as you progress along your journey. With the right mindset, knowledge, and tools, you can go from zero to hero and achieve the financial success you desire. - Adella Pasos